The Gigging Guitarist

Traditional Hymns and Spirituals For Fingerstyle Guitar

Arranged for Guitar By Michael Wood

THE

GIGGING

Table of Contents

<u>Performance Notes</u>

- Every attempt was made to eliminate awkward fingerings and motions, especially on the quicker tunes. Slurs should be followed. Careful attention was given to these instances and these slurs are important to the overall fingering and flow of the tune.

- Some tunes use tenuto marks. These are meant to indicate the melodic notes and more emphasis should be placed on these notes.

- Optional introductions are listed for tunes without written introductions.

2

This page left intentionally blank.

OLD HUNDREDTH

(DOXOLOGY)

Louis Bourgeois (1551)
Arr. Michael Wood

VERY FREELY
NO CHORDS

CROWN HIM WITH MANY CROWNS

MATTHEW BRIDGES (1800 – 1894)
TUNE: DIADEMATA BY GEORGE J. ELVEY (1816 – 1893)
ARR. MICHAEL WOOD

TENDERLY

* OPTIONAL INTRO

Be Thou My Vision
(Slane)

Traditional Irish Hymn
Arr. Michael Wood

* OPTIONAL INTRO

This Is My Father's World

(Terra Beata)

Words by Maltbie Babcock (1858 – 1901)
Traditional English Tune
Arr. Michael Wood

WHAT A FRIEND WE HAVE IN JESUS

WORDS BY JOSEPH SCRIVEN (1819 – 1886)
MUSIC BY CHARLES CONVERSE (1832 – 1918)
ARR. MICHAEL WOOD

SOMBERLY

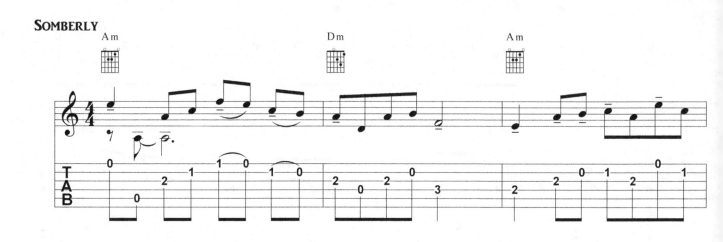

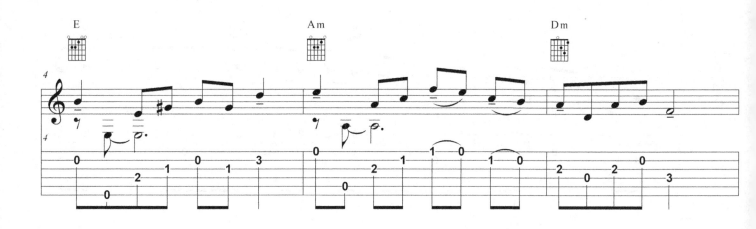

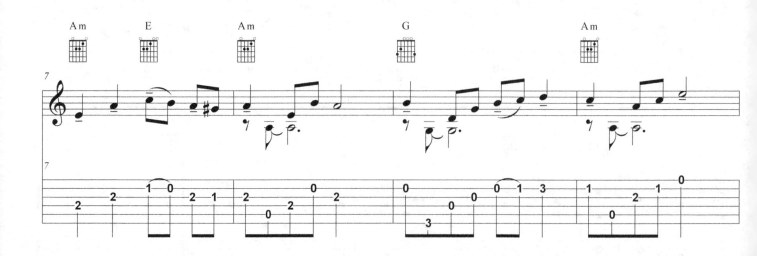

COME THOU FOUNT OF EVERY BLESSING

ROBERT ROBINSON (1758)
ARR. MICHAEL WOOD

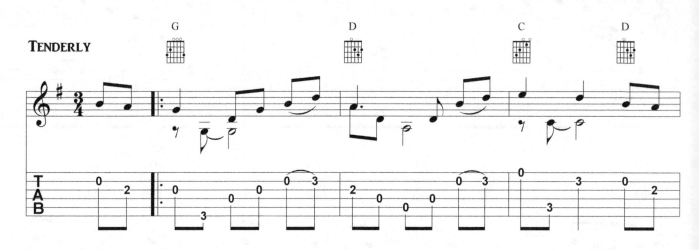

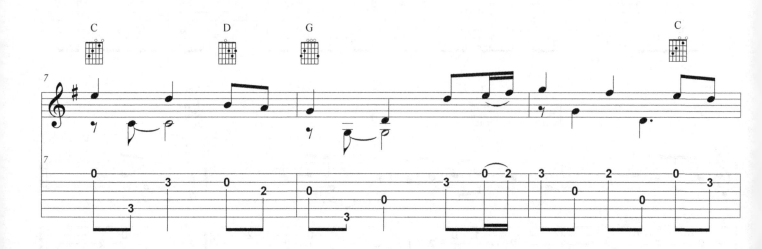

Simple Gifts

Traditional Shaker Hymn
Joseph Brackett (1797 – 1882)
Arr. Michael Wood

AMAZING GRACE

TRADITIONAL
ARR. MICHAEL WOOD

16

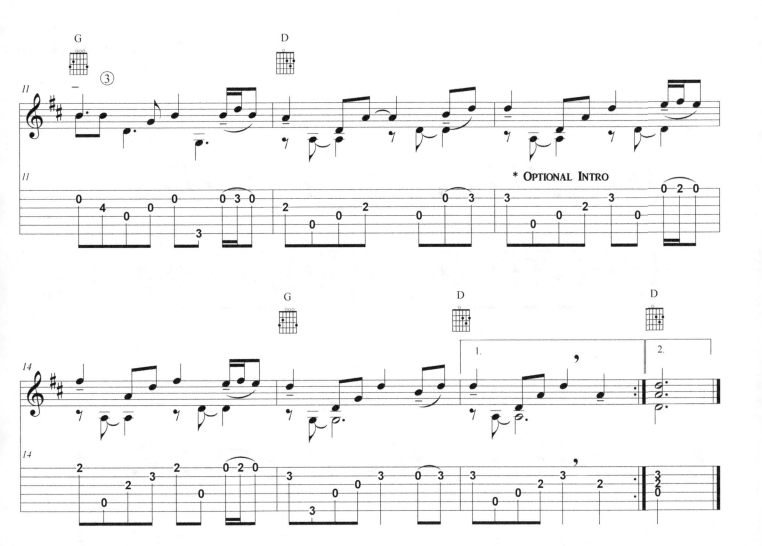

* Optional Intro

WHAT WONDROUS LOVE IS THIS

ANONYMOUS
ARR. MICHAEL WOOD

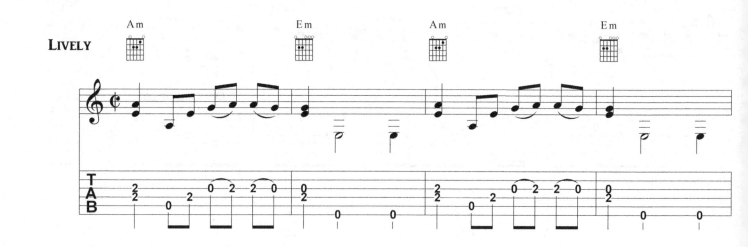

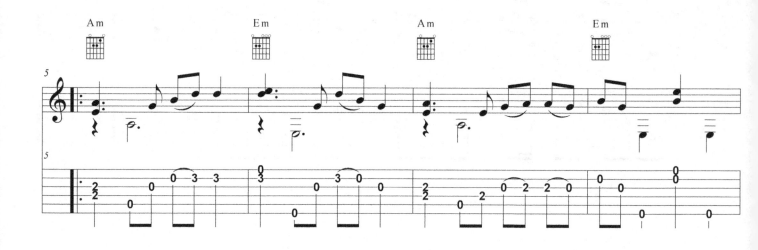

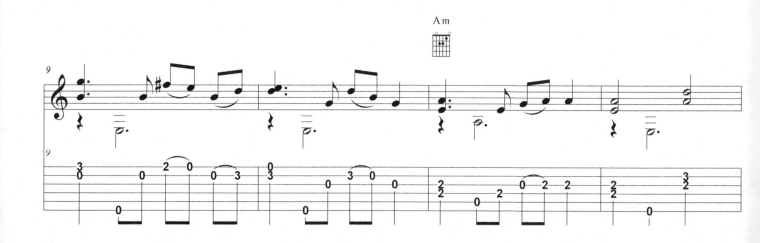

It Is Well With My Soul

(When Peace, Like a River)

Words by Horatio Gates Spafford (1828 – 1888)
Tune: Ville du Havre by Philip Bliss (1838 – 1876)
Arr. Michael Wood

* OPTIONAL
INTRO

O For a Thousand Tongues To Sing

Charles Wesley (1707 – 1788)
Arr. Michael Wood

How Firm a Foundation

24

ATTRIBUTED TO SEVERAL AUTHORS
ARR. MICHAEL WOOD

© 2017 MICHAEL WOOD

Abide with Me
(Eventide)

Henry Francis Lyte (1793 – 1847)
Arr. Michael Wood

Down to the River to Pray

Trad. American Spiritual
Arr. Michael Wood

SWEET HOUR OF PRAYER

MUSIC BY W. W. WALFORD (1772 – 1850)
TUNE: SWEET HOUR OF PRAYER, SWEET HOUR OF PRAYER
BY WILLIAM B. BRADBURY (1816 – 1868)
ARR. MICHAEL WOOD

HE LEADETH ME

WILLIAM BRADBUY (1816 - 1868)
ARR. MICHAEL WOOD

* OPTIONAL INTRO

Wayfaring Stranger

American Folk
Arr. Michael Wood

* OPTIONAL INTRO

About The Author

Dr. Michael Wood graduated in 2012 from the University of North Carolina at Greensboro with a doctorate in music performance and a certificate in ethnomusicology. While researching for his dissertation on the hammered dulcimer in Appalachian Old Time music, Michael became immersed in the wealth of wonderful and rich traditions of Old Time and Celtic music. While learning more about this music, he quickly became adept at the hammered dulcimer, mountain dulcimer (also known as Appalachian or lap dulcimer), and guitar. Originally focusing on classical guitar literature, Michael has since combined the style, techniques, and repertoire for dulcimer, banjo, and classical guitar to create his own unique approach to fingerstyle guitar music.

Michael also graduated from the University of Oklahoma with a masters in music performance and the University of North Carolina at Greensboro with a bachelor's degree in music education. He currently lives in Greensboro, North Carolina with his wife Sara, son Jamie, and daughter Eliza. He and his wife regularly perform on a unique blend of instruments including Michael on guitar, hammered dulcimer, mountain dulcimer, marimba, vibraphone, cajón, djembe, and other percussion instruments, as well as Sara on hammered dulcimer, mountain dulcimer, flute, piano, tin whistle, marimba, and vibraphone.

More information can be found at **www.EdgeOfTheWorldMusic.com** as well as **www.MichaelAlanWood.com**

About the Book

Intended for gigging musicians, the tunes in this book were arranged with a number of special considerations in mind. First and foremost, these tunes were arranged to be played easily. They are not necessarily easy as far as difficulty goes, but these arrangements use voice leadings and motions that reduce awkward hand positions and stretches that could cause hand fatigue or hand issues down the line. All arrangements are in standard tuning (E A D G B E). These arrangements were deliberately kept to a maximum of two pages to eliminate pages turns while performing. All tunes can be repeated, at the player's discretion, any number of times. Introductions and endings are noted sparsely to both save space and allow the performer to add his or her own introductions and endings.

One thing you will also notice is that there are no full barre chords in this book, as barre chords place a lot of stress on a player's hands. There are a few instances of half barre chords (top three strings only), but even these are used sparingly. These arrangements utilize drones when appropriate and bass notes are frequently offset from strong beats (e.g. bass notes landing on the *and* of the beat rather than *on* the beat). Although this style differs from many other guitar arrangements, this method of playing emphasizes the melody and allows the long, held bass notes (often open strings when possible) to fill out the soundscape. You'll find that rhythm is utilized to create a wonderfully full texture, rather than stacked notes as found in other guitar arrangements. This again is for the ease of reading and playability for the performer. As you become more comfortable with these arrangements, you will find areas where you could easily thicken the texture with some additional notes as you see fit. This book serves as a basic guide with endless possible embellishments and additions available to the performer.

Made in the USA
Monee, IL
16 June 2024

59967841R00024